SAVING EARTH'S BIOMES
PROTECTING THE AMAZON RAINFOREST

by Tracy Vonder Brink

FOCUS READERS

NAVIGATOR

WWW.FOCUSREADERS.COM

Focus Readers is distributed by North Star Editions:
sales@northstareditions.com | 888-417-0195

Produced for Focus Readers by Red Line Editorial.

Content Consultant: Eve Bratman, Assistant Professor of Environmental Studies, Franklin & Marshall College

Photographs ©: Aleksandr_Vorobev/iStockphoto, cover, 1; FG Trade/iStockphoto, 4–5; drmakkoy/iStockphoto, 7; Cris Bouroncle/AFP/Getty Images, 9; aniroot/iStockphoto, 11; Enjoylife2/iStockphoto, 12–13; Kalistratova/iStockphoto, 15; luoman/iStockphoto, 17, 24–25; Jesse Allen/NASA, 18–19 (top), 18–19 (bottom); Zé Barretta/iStockphoto, 21; Red Line Editorial, 22; Dolores Ochoa/AP Images, 27; Desiree Stover/NASA, 29

Library of Congress Cataloging-in-Publication Data
Names: Vonder Brink, Tracy, author.
Title: Protecting the Amazon rainforest / by Tracy Vonder Brink.
Description: Lake Elmo, MN : Focus Readers, [2020] | Series: Saving earth's
   biomes | Includes index. | Audience: Grades 4-6
Identifiers: LCCN 2019025958 (print) | LCCN 2019025959 (ebook) | ISBN
   9781644930687 (hardcover) | ISBN 9781644931479 (paperback) | ISBN
   9781644933053 (ebook pdf) | ISBN 9781644932261 (hosted ebook)
Subjects: LCSH: Rain forest conservation--Amazon River Region--Juvenile
   literature. | Environmental protection--Amazon River Region--Juvenile
   literature.
Classification: LCC SD414.A43 V66 2020 (print) | LCC SD414.A43 (ebook) |
   DDC 333.75/1609811--dc23
LC record available at https://lccn.loc.gov/2019025958
LC ebook record available at https://lccn.loc.gov/2019025959

Printed in the United States of America
Mankato, MN
012020

ABOUT THE AUTHOR

Tracy Vonder Brink loves writing true stories for young readers. She has never visited the Amazon rainforest but would like to see it someday, especially if she could see some of its big spiders. Tracy lives in Ohio with her husband, two daughters, and two rescue dogs.

TABLE OF CONTENTS

CHAPTER 1

TROUBLE IN THE AMAZON

The Amazon is the largest rainforest on Earth. Most of the rainforest is in Brazil. But it stretches across nine countries. Millions of **species** live in the Amazon rainforest. Many of these plants and animals are not found anywhere else on Earth. One example is the Amazon river dolphin.

The Amazon is home to one of Earth's longest rivers, the Amazon River.

The original residents and caretakers of the Amazon have lived there for thousands of years. For many years, some of these **indigenous** tribes lived in large settlements. Others lived in small communities. People in these tribes learned which plants were good to eat. They used many plants for medicines, too. They planted fruit trees. They cleared small amounts of land to grow crops. In addition, they hunted and fished only as much as they needed. As a result, the rainforest stayed healthy.

In the 1500s, explorers and **missionaries** from Europe came to South America. They killed many of the indigenous people living there. Later, they brought enslaved people from Africa. The Europeans also formed settlements.

AMAZON RAINFOREST

VENEZUELA GUYANA SURINAME FRENCH GUIANA
COLOMBIA
ECUADOR
AMAZON RAINFOREST
PERU BRAZIL
BOLIVIA

N
W E
S

SOUTH AMERICA

People from other countries moved to the Amazon, too. Today, more than 30 million people live in the region.

At first, Europeans mined the Amazon for gold. Then they learned the forest held other riches. They cut down mahogany trees for their wood. They also hunted animals, such as jaguars, for their fur.

INDIGENOUS TRIBES

Approximately 400 indigenous tribes live in the Amazon rainforest. Most of these tribes live in small villages. Many tribes have contact with outsiders. But as many as 100 tribes avoid contact with the outside world. All of these tribes are at risk. When the rainforest is cut down, they lose their homes.

An illegal gold mining camp sits in a deforested area of Peru.

Over time, companies and farmers cleared away more of the Amazon's trees. The land is mostly used for farms and cattle ranches. Some land is for mining. More than 20 percent of the Amazon has already been cleared. For many reasons, this **deforestation** is a major problem for the rainforest and the planet.

THE AMAZON RIVER DOLPHIN

Unlike other dolphins, Amazon river dolphins do not live in the ocean. They live in rainforest rivers. Young river dolphins are gray. But they turn pink as they grow older.

Amazon river dolphins can turn their heads farther than other dolphins. This ability helps them swim around tree trunks. They can even swim upside down. These dolphins have longer snouts, too. Their long snouts help them dig through mud and catch fish.

However, waste from gold mines pollutes many Amazon rivers. The waste poisons the fish that dolphins eat. When dolphins eat poisoned fish, they become sick.

Every 10 years, the number of Amazon river dolphins is cut in half.

Scientists are studying these dolphins. They want to find out how many live in the rainforest's rivers. They want to learn if the dolphins are healthy. They also want to know where exactly these dolphins live. This information will help people protect Amazon river dolphins.

CHAPTER 2

DEFORESTATION DAMAGE

The Amazon rainforest is home to many types of plants and animals. This variety of species is known as biodiversity. Each species plays a different role in the Amazon's many **ecosystems**. If species die out, the rainforest's health will suffer. People will suffer as well.

Golden lion tamarins are among the thousands of endangered species in the Amazon.

Deforestation is a major threat to life in the Amazon. When trees are cut down, plants die. Animals lose their homes, too. Many animals can live in only one kind of **habitat**. If that habitat disappears, those animals may die out completely.

In addition, the Amazon depends on its trees. Tree roots suck up water from the ground. Sunlight heats the trees' leaves. Then the leaves give off steam. The steam collects and forms clouds. The clouds make rain. Rainwater enters the ground. The cycle begins again. Without this cycle, the Amazon would be a desert.

However, deforestation has led to fewer trees in the Amazon. And the loss of trees

Scientists often call the Amazon's massive cloud system a river in the sky.

has led to less rain. Between 2005 and 2018, three droughts hit the Amazon. These periods of little rain made it harder for many species to survive. They also made life harder for people living in the Amazon. These people depend on water for everything from bathing to fishing.

Deforestation harms more than just the Amazon. It harms the entire planet. That is because plants help remove carbon dioxide from the air. When the rainforest is cut down, fewer plants can take carbon dioxide out of the air. In addition, trees store carbon in their wood. Cutting down trees releases that carbon into the air.

CARBON DIOXIDE

Many vehicles, such as cars and airplanes, burn fuel for energy. When fuel is burned, carbon dioxide enters the air. Carbon dioxide is a gas that traps heat. Having some of this gas in the air is good. It helps keep the planet warm. But too much carbon dioxide is harmful. It leads to **climate change**.

In 2018, the Amazon lost an area nearly the size of Hawaii to deforestation.

High levels of carbon dioxide in the air are causing climate change. And this global crisis is changing the world's weather patterns. Many experts believe that climate change is the biggest threat to life on Earth.

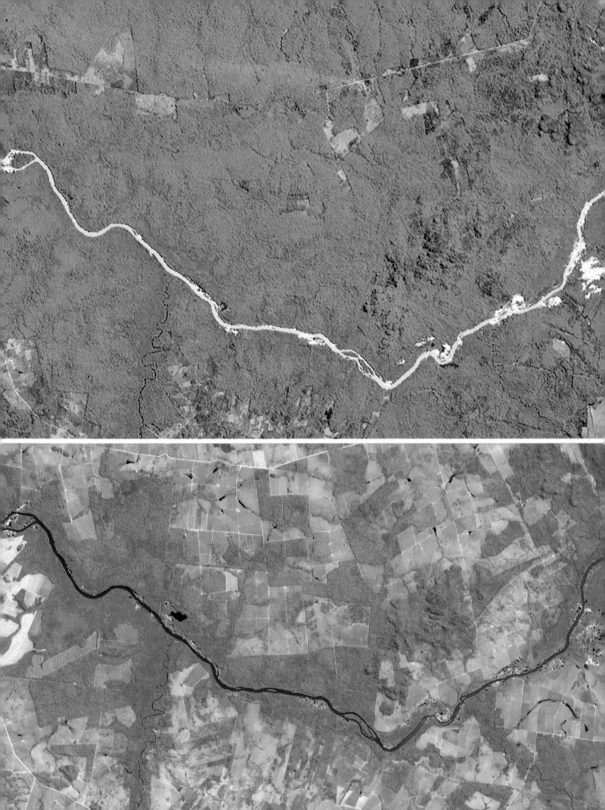

CHAPTER 3

HEALING THE RAINFOREST

To help the Amazon rainforest, scientists try to learn which parts are in danger. For example, they make maps of the Amazon. They often use satellites to take pictures from space. These pictures show how much of the rainforest has already been destroyed. They also show how the Amazon is changing.

Satellite images show deforestation in one part of the Amazon from 1992 (top) to 2006 (bottom).

In addition, some countries have marked certain rainforest areas as reserves. These places are protected to keep life there safe. The countries decide what type of reserve each area will be. For example, some areas are national parks.

NATURAL GOODS

In 1988, Brazil created a new type of reserve. In this area, local tribes can gather and sell natural rainforest goods. These items can be gathered without cutting down trees. Some examples are rubber, brazil nuts, and açaí (ah-sah-*ee*) berries. Over time, the demand for these goods has grown. Local people can make more and more money from these goods. As a result, fewer trees are cut down for farms and ranches.

An indigenous worker harvests a branch of açaí berries.

In some reserves, farming and logging are banned. In others, those activities are limited. Local tribes also control some reserves. One kind of reserve lets tribes gather and sell natural rainforest goods.

Reserves help guard the land. Rules about how the land is used protect the plants and animals there. These rules

PROTECTED AND INDIGENOUS AREAS OF THE AMAZON

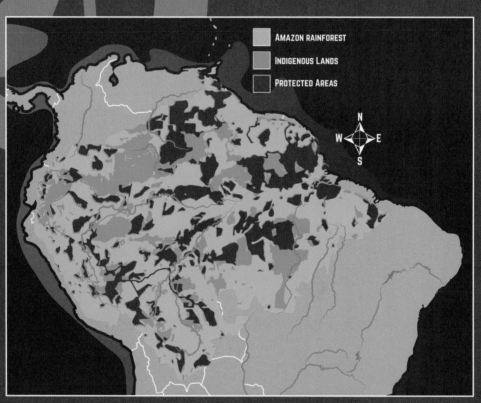

AMAZON RAINFOREST

INDIGENOUS LANDS

PROTECTED AREAS

also help the people who depend on the Amazon for their ways of life. However, the leaders of countries change. New leaders sometimes change how reserves can be used. Those changes may cause more trees to be cut down.

In addition, many parts of the Amazon have already been cleared. Reserves cannot help these areas. In response, one organization started a program to plant new trees. So far, workers have planted seeds for approximately three million new trees. The group planned to plant 70 million more by 2023. However, those parts of the rainforest could take thousands of years to grow back fully.

CHAPTER 4

LOOKING AHEAD

The Amazon rainforest continues to be in danger. For example, a new leader took power in Brazil in 2019. This leader supported more mining and farming in the rainforest. He also supported opening up indigenous land to these activities. Not surprisingly, deforestation in Brazil got worse in 2019.

Between 2012 and 2018, deforestation in Brazil rose by more than 70 percent.

Even so, other parts of the Amazon are being helped. In 2018, Peru decided to create a new national park. And Colombia made one of its parks larger. The park set a record for the world's largest tropical rainforest national park.

Indigenous tribes have also joined together. These tribes are working to get countries to help the Amazon. More than 400 different groups are working to support indigenous rights. They are trying to create a reserve the size of Mexico. Some tribes also patrol the reserves. They report any illegal logging.

In addition, ecotours teach people about the rainforest. These types of tours

In 2019, members of the Waorani tribe marched after winning a lawsuit to prevent oil digging on their land.

try to have little impact on natural areas. The tours help local communities, too. Visitors pay these communities to guide them through the rainforest. The visitors learn about protecting it.

Buying natural rainforest goods helps the Amazon, too. Companies can work to increase demand for these goods. When that happens, more rainforest may be protected to support those businesses.

Scientists continue to study the Amazon. In 2018, scientists sent a new piece of equipment into space. For two years, this equipment took pictures of Earth's rainforests. It also created 3D maps of the rainforests. The maps showed details both above and below the trees' leaves. Using these maps, scientists can understand how much carbon dioxide is entering the air. Then they can make better plans for reducing those levels.

A scientist inspects a piece of the equipment used to take pictures of rainforests from space.

Much more needs to be done to help the Amazon. Companies and farmers are still clearing trees. And climate change remains a massive danger. However, many people and groups around the world care about the Amazon. They will keep working to protect the rainforest.

FOCUS ON
PROTECTING THE AMAZON RAINFOREST

Write your answers on a separate piece of paper.

1. Write a letter to a friend describing what you learned about buying natural goods from the rainforest.

2. Do you think current efforts to protect the Amazon are enough? Why or why not?

3. What is one way deforestation affects the Amazon?
   A. It makes space for more reserves.
   B. It makes droughts more likely.
   C. It makes space for more ecotourism.

4. What might happen if most of the Amazon rainforest becomes replanted and protected?
   A. The rainforest might help slow climate change.
   B. The rainforest might provide more trees for logging.
   C. The rainforest might lose its biodiversity.

Answer key on page 32.

GLOSSARY

climate change
A human-caused global crisis involving long-term changes in Earth's temperature and weather patterns.

deforestation
The removal of the trees in a forest, usually by cutting or burning.

ecosystems
Communities of living things and how they interact with their surrounding environments.

habitat
The type of place where plants or animals normally grow or live.

indigenous
Native to a region, or belonging to ancestors who did not immigrate to the region.

missionaries
People who teach religious beliefs and attempt to convince others of those beliefs.

species
Groups of animals or plants that share the same body shape and can breed with one another.

TO LEARN MORE

BOOKS

Harris, Duchess. *Environmental Protests.* Minneapolis: Abdo Publishing, 2018.

Iyer, Rani. *Endangered Rain Forests: Investigating Rain Forests in Crisis.* North Mankato, MN: Capstone Press, 2015.

Rector, Rebecca Kraft. *The Amazon Rainforest.* Lake Elmo, MN: Focus Readers, 2018.

NOTE TO EDUCATORS

Visit **www.focusreaders.com** to find lesson plans, activities, links, and other resources related to this title.

INDEX

Answer Key: 1. Answers will vary; **2.** Answers will vary; **3.** B; **4.** A